The
Synagogue

House of the Jewish People

by Susan Van Dusen
and Rabbi Marc Berkson

BEHRMAN HOUSE

And let them make me a sanctuary

that I may dwell among them.

EXODUS 25:8

To my husband, George, my children, Danny and

David, and my parents, Jack and Adelyn Nixon…

— SVD

And to my wife, Deborah Carter, and

my children, Michal, Abigail, and Jesse…

— MB

…who share with us in the life of the synagogue.

Book Design: Howard Levy Design

Artists: Matt Collins (cover, pages 10, 18-19, 70, 91, 94) and Larry Nolte

The authors and publisher gratefully acknowledge the following sources of photographs and art for this book:

Creative Image: 5, 9, 36 (top and bottom), 37 (center left and center right), 38, 40, 42 (bottom), 43 (top), 45 (bottom), 49, 51, 56 (top right, bottom right), 57 (center), 59, 62, 66, 75, 76, 82, 83, 84, 85 (top); **Gustov Doré:** 16; **SuperStock:** 17, 73; **United Synagogue Review/Adath Israel Congregation:** 27; **Kulterinstitute:** 30 (top); **The Society of Friends of Touro Synagogue/ National Historic Shrine, Inc.:** 31 (bottom right); **Beth Hatefutsoth, The Nahum Goldmann Museum of the Jewish Diaspora, Tel Aviv:** 31 (top left); **Frank Darmstaedter:** 31 (bottom left); Richard Lobell: 31 (top right), 60 (bottom), 81; Bill Aron: 35, 41; **Jewish Theological Seminary, Womens League Seminary Synagogue. Photo: Marjorie Gersten:** 36 (center left); **Klein Brothers:** 36 (center right), 39, 45; **Hebrew Union College-Jewish Institute of Religion:** 37 (bottom), 40 (top), 56 (bottom left), 60 (top); **George E. Ernst:** 40 (bottom); **Gila Gevirtz:** 43 (bottom); **Francene Keery:** 45 (top), 57 (bottom), 58 (top), 65, 72; **Israel Ministry of Tourism:** 74; **Creative Image/Temple Emeth, Teaneck, NJ:** 79; **Sunny Yellen:** 85 (bottom)\

Library of Congress Cataloging-in-Publication Data
Van Dusan, Susan
        The synagogue: house of the Jewish people/Susan Van Dusen, Marc Berkson.
            p. cm.
        Summary: Discusses the history and significance of the synagogue as a gathering place for
            Jews. Includes activities and discussion questions.
            ISBN 0-87441-664-7
        1. Synagogues juvenile literature. [1. Synagogues. 2. Judaism-Customs and practices.] I.
            Berkson, Marc. II. Title
        BM653.V36 1999
        296.6'5--dc21

Published by Behrman House

MANUFACTURED IN THE UNITED STATES OF AMERICA

Contents

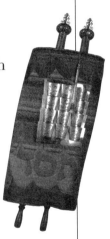

INTRODUCTION

Our Home Away From Home

Have you ever felt God's presence when you pray in your synagogue sanctuary? Are you delighted by the sweet taste of the hamantashen your temple serves on Purim? Does learning a new Hebrew prayer in your religious school make you feel proud and grown-up? What other good experiences have you had in the synagogue?

We learn how to pray and to read Hebrew in the synagogue's religious school.

A synagogue is a holy place for the Jewish people. It is a place where all Jews are welcome to join in prayer, study, and celebration. The synagogue is our home away from home. It is a place where we go to meet old friends and make new ones. We go for good times, such as bat mitzvah celebrations, and for good works, such as collecting food for the hungry. Why do you think the Jewish community has created this special place? Would it be just as good to meet in a park, or a mall, or a skating rink? Why is it important that we meet in our own special place?

As you read this book, you will learn why and how the Jewish people came to build synagogues. You will learn the importance of the holy objects in synagogues, the prayer clothing we wear, and the people who work in synagogues. You will learn how synagogues strengthen us and help us to connect with our tradition and our community. And you will learn how you can contribute your own strength to make the synagogue of the future even stronger.

Where Our Ancestors First Worshipped

Jews do many things together in the synagogue. We pray, learn Hebrew, and study Torah in the synagogue. We also celebrate weddings, births, Shabbat, and holidays, such as Sukkot and Shavuot, in the synagogue. And we organize clothing drives for the needy and hold cooking classes, book fairs, concerts, and chess tournaments in the synagogue.

But how did the synagogue come to be? How did our ancestors choose one place to do all these things? Let us travel back in time to the beginnings of the Jewish people.

EARLY PLACES OF WORSHIP

Four thousand years ago, our ancestors were frightened and confused by the many natural events they could not understand or control. They saw electric bolts of lightning that seemed to split the sky, and they heard the deafening rumble of thunder. They watched the sun set each evening, uncertain that it would rise again in the morning. And they saw the seasons change from spring to summer to fall to winter, and then back to spring again. Our ancestors understood that no man or woman could make these things happen. They also understood that a power beyond anything they could see, hear, touch, or smell must be responsible for creating the many wonders of nature. In time, they came to understand that the power is God.

Our ancestors wanted to talk to God. They wanted to thank God for all the good God had given them and to tell God about their hopes, happiness, worries, and sadness. They began by worshipping in places where they felt God's spirit.

How would you feel if suddenly the sky were *under* your feet and the sea floated *above* your head? It feels good to know that there is order in the world around us, to feel the ground firmly under us, and to know the sun will rise each morning and the moon and stars will light the night sky above. Our tradition teaches us to thank God for these wonders of nature and for all the goodness in Creation.

For example, they worshipped God on high mountains that seemed to reach up toward the heavens, and they worshipped God in the wilderness whose dry, dusty land stretched around them for miles. In these early times, there was no one place where our people came together to worship.

BECOMING A FREE PEOPLE

The Torah tells us that there was a famine in Canaan, the land where our ancestors lived. In those days, our people—who were called the children of Israel, or Israelites—moved to Egypt to find food. At first, there was plenty for all. The Egyptians and Israelites lived together in peace. But later, a cruel king, known as Pharaoh, arose. Pharaoh, who ruled over Egypt, feared that our people would become strong and join Egypt's enemies. So, he enslaved our ancestors, and their lives were filled with suffering.

Then, the Torah teaches, God heard the cries of the Israelites and told Moses to lead them out of Egypt. After centuries in Egypt, the Israelites left Egypt to become a free people who could serve God instead of Pharaoh. They crossed the Sea of Reeds and began their journey through the wilderness. When they set up camp at the foot of Mount Sinai, God spoke to Moses, saying, "Come up to Me." And Moses went up the mountain to speak with God.

Judaism teaches us to live as creatures made in God's image. This does not mean that we look like God. It means that we can act in God's ways. Just as the Torah teaches us that God heard the cries of the Israelite slaves and helped them, so we can pay attention to the cries of those in need. These synagogue members are collecting food for the hungry. What else can members of a synagogue do to help those in need?

ORAH'S STORY

Hi! I'm Orah. I'm ten years old. Every day I trudge, with my family
and friends, through the wilderness. We are following Moses, who
is leading us to the Land of Israel, the Promised Land.

There is no time to play and little time to rest. During the day,
we broil in the burning sun, and at night, our teeth chatter from
the freezing cold. There is never enough water. Dust is every-
where, even in our food! Now we have made our camp around
a mountain called Mount Sinai. Moses told us that he will meet
with God at the top. So, he climbed up
the mountain, and we haven't
seen him for weeks. I feel
lonely and scared.

Moses told us there is
only one God. I wonder
if he will bring back
something from God.
What could such a gift be?
I hope Moses returns soon.

I miss Moses. I'm afraid we
will never see him again and
that we will be stuck in this
wilderness forever. But I will
wait for Moses, and I will pray
to God for his safe return.

MOSES RETURNS

The Torah tells us that, after forty days and nights, Moses came down from the top of Mount Sinai. He brought back two stone tablets with God's commandments—the Ten Commandments—written on them.

THE TEN COMMANDMENTS

1. I am Adonai your GOD, who brought you out of the land of Egypt.
2. Do not worship any other gods. Do not worship idols.
3. Do not swear falsely by the name of Adonai, your GOD.
4. Remember Shabbat and keep it holy.
5. Honor your father and mother.
6. Do not murder.
7. Do not take another person's wife or husband.
8. Do not steal.
9. Do not tell lies about another person.
10. Do not wish to own what belongs to someone else.

Moses told the children of Israel that God said: "Let them build Me a sanctuary that I may dwell among them."

God asked the children of Israel to build a sanctuary on earth where God could dwell among them and where the Jewish people could gather together. Read all about it in a special edition of *The Ancient Times*.

WHAT DO YOU THINK?

Do you think that God was actually going to live in the Tent of Meeting? Why or why not? Why do you think our people were asked to build God a dwelling place on earth?

The Ancient Times

The fifth month of the first year after the Exodus from Egypt

Moses Back on Track — with Special Orders from God

Having safely returned from Mount Sinai with the two tablets of the Ten Commandments, Moses now reports that we are to "build a sanctuary so that God may dwell among us."

The sanctuary is a holy place where the spirit of God will be present and where the children of Israel are welcome to seek God.

WEATHER REPORT
Blistering heat, very low humidity

The Ancient Times

Plans and More Plans!

Shortly after his arrival, Moses explained the detailed plans for the sanctuary. The plans include an ark—the *Aron Kodesh*—to hold the tablets of the Ten Commandments, as well as a tent of meeting called the *Ohel Mo'ed*. The *Aron Kodesh* will be housed within the *Ohel Mo'ed*.

The *Aron Kodesh* and the *Ohel Mo'ed* will be portable—that is, possible to carry while the Israelites continue their journey to the Promised Land.

Bezalel to Head New Projects

Master craftsman Bezalel was chosen to direct the new building projects. "The plans are quite clear," he said. "Construction will begin immediately."

Building Material Shortage

The following material is needed for construction of the *Aron Kodesh* and *Ohel Mo'ed*: goat hair, tanned ram skins, acacia wood, gold, silver, copper. Anyone willing to donate these materials, please contact Moses.

Mystery

Answer the questions below by filling in the blank spaces. Read the letters in the circles from top to bottom to discover the secret word.

1. What mountain did Moses climb to talk with God?

Mount ◯ _ _ _ _

2. What were the Israelites in ancient Egypt?

_ _ ◯ _ _ _ _

3. How many gods do the Jewish people worship?

_ _ ◯ _

4. What was carved into the stone tablets Moses brought down from Mount Sinai? ◯ _ _ _ _ _ _ _ _ _ _

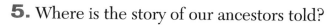

5. Where is the story of our ancestors told?

◯ _ _ _ _

6. What makes the wilderness so warm?

_ ◯ _

7. What are the Hebrew words for the place where the Ten Commandments were kept? ◯ _ _ _ _ _ _ _ _ _

8. How many days was Moses on Mount Sinai?

_ _ ◯ _ _ _

9. Where did Pharaoh rule?

_ _ ◯ _ _

What is the mystery word?

_____

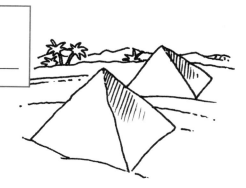

The Holy Temple

Ａs the children of Israel journeyed to the Land
of Israel, they carried the Tent of Meeting, the Ohel
Mo'ed, with them. Once there, it continued to be at
the center of their worship service until Jerusalem
was conquered and the Holy Temple was built. In
this chapter, you will learn who built the Temple and
how the children of Israel worshipped there. You will
also learn who destroyed the Temple and how Judaism
survived this great loss.

KING DAVID AND THE TEMPLE

The children of Israel carried the *Ohel Mo'ed* with them across the Sinai Wilderness into the Promised Land. They stopped from time to time and set up the Tent of Meeting in several different places, but there was no permanent place for Jews to pray to God.

The children of Israel cross the Jordan River into the Land of Israel. After forty years of wandering through the wilderness, the Israelites could now worship God in their own land.

After King David conquered Jerusalem, he decided to create a permanent home there for the *Aron Kodesh,* the Holy Ark. He bought land on Mount Moriah upon which to build the Holy Temple. But the Bible teaches that God would not allow David to build the Temple because he had fought many wars and had shed much blood.

Instead, David's son Solomon was given the privilege of building God's house.

King David was disappointed that he could not build the Temple, *Beit Hamikdash,* but he accepted God's will and helped to collect the materials that would be used to construct it.

WHAT DO YOU THINK?

Why do you think God did not want a warrior to build the Temple? What kind of person would you want to build a place where you, your family, and your friends would come to pray? Why?

BUILDING THE FIRST TEMPLE

שָׁלוֹם
shalom
peace

During King Solomon's reign, Israel was at peace with its neighbors. In fact, Solomon's name in Hebrew, *Shlomo*, comes from the word *shalom*, שָׁלוֹם, which means "peace."

Solomon was very wise. He understood that the Temple was not going to be a house for God to live in, because God did not need a place to sleep or to eat. Instead, he built a place to honor God, a place where people could feel close to God.

An ancient legend explains how the location of the Holy Temple was chosen.

Jewish tradition teaches the importance of living peacefully—at home, at school, at play, and at work. Why do you think these boys were fighting? What could they have done instead of fighting?

A FOUNDATION OF LOVING-KINDNESS

Long ago, in the days of King Solomon, two brothers had a farm on the outskirts of Jerusalem. One brother had six children. The other had none. Year after year, the brothers shared their harvest of wheat.

One autumn night, the younger brother lay in bed thinking: *My brother has so many mouths to feed. It is not fair that he receives only half the harvest of our field.* So he rose from his bed and took three bundles of wheat from his portion and placed them with his brother's.

That very night, his brother tossed and turned in his bed. *My brother has no children to provide for him when he is old. It is not fair that he receives only half the harvest.* So he rose from his bed and took three bundles of his wheat and placed them with his brother's portion.

In the morning, both brothers were astounded to find their piles of wheat just as they had been the day before.

Each night of the harvest, the two brought a portion of their wheat one to the other. And, each morning, they found their piles of wheat remained as they had been at nightfall.

One night, the two brothers happened to meet in the middle of the hill, each carrying wheat for the other. Understanding what had happened, they put down the bundles of wheat and embraced.

When the time came to build the Holy Temple, God led King
Solomon to the hill. "This is where you shall build My Holy
Temple. For the Temple must be built on a foundation of loving-
kindness." And so the *Beit Hamikdash* was built on the very spot
where the brothers embraced.

WHY WAS THE TEMPLE SO PRECIOUS?

Among the many reasons why the Temple was so precious to the Jewish people was:

1. *It was the first permanent place where the Jewish people could come together to worship God.*

Jews came from all over the Land of Israel, and even from outside the Land, to worship at the Temple. They celebrated festivals with family and friends, and they learned about God's commandments.

2. *The Israelites thanked God for the good in their lives by offering sacrifices in the Holy Temple.*

Our ancestors understood that all the goodness in our lives is a gift from God. The wheat from which we make bread is a gift from God. The milk from cows is a gift from God. Even the air and water we breathe and drink are gifts from

Did You Know?

When the Temple priests asked for God's blessings for our people, they put their hands in the form of the letter *shin* (שׁ — see the illustration on the left) because *shin* is the first letter of one of God's names, Shaddai. For the same reason, you will find the letter *shin* on almost every mezuzah case.

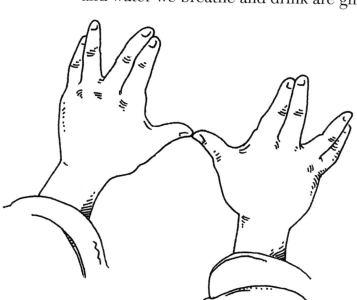

God. In order to thank God for these many gifts, Temple priests offered daily sacrifices of food, drink, and animals at the *Beit Hamikdash*. In addition, the priests offered sacrifices to God from those who wanted to apologize for having sinned.

Our ancestors journeyed three times a year—on the festivals of Passover, Shavuot, and Sukkot—to offer sacrifices at the Temple in Jerusalem.

WHAT DO YOU THINK?

The ancient rabbis suggested another name for God that begins with the letter *shin*. It is Shalom, שָׁלוֹם. Do you think that is a good name for God? Why or why not?

THE FIRST SYNAGOGUES

The First Temple was built almost three thousand years ago in about 960 BCE by King Solomon. In 586 BCE the Babylonians, who were ruled by King Nebuchadnezzar, conquered Jerusalem, destroyed the Temple, and captured many Jews whom they sent to the ancient land of Babylonia. And so, our ancestors lost their central place of worship. Babylonia was hundreds of miles away from Israel. How could our people continue to worship God? How could they continue to live as Jews?

This ancient stone sculpture shows a Jewish family that was forced to leave Israel after the destruction of the Temple.

Did You Know?

Babylonia is where the modern country of Iraq is today. Can you find Iraq on a world map? Israel? Imagine traveling the distance between these two countries in the time before planes. Do you think you might feel homesick for Israel if you lived in Babylonia?

Although no one knows for certain where the first synagogues were built, they may have been built by the Jews of Babylonia. No longer able to gather at the Temple, they formed small communities whose main purpose was prayer and the study of God's word. In such communities, prayer replaced the animal sacrifices of the Temple.

This is a model of the city of Jerusalem before the destruction of the Second Temple. The Holy of Holies — a small room in the Temple, where the *Aron Kodesh* was placed — is shown on the right.

Just before the holidays of Sukkot, Passover, and Shavuot, Jews throughout Israel and nearby countries would travel to Jerusalem. On the holiday, they gathered at the Temple to pray and to perform sacrifices.

THE SECOND TEMPLE

Our people vowed to return to Jerusalem and rebuild the Temple. And that is what happened. The Second Temple stood in Jerusalem from about 515 BCE to 70 CE. King Herod was the last to do construction on the Temple. He increased its size and beauty, using great white stones. The largest stone that remains is 30 feet long and weighs over 200 tons.

Although our ancestors offered sacrifices in the Temple in Jerusalem, they now also took part in local prayer services throughout Israel. The Talmud tells us that there were one hundred synagogues in Jerusalem in the days of the Second Temple.

In 70 CE the Romans conquered Jerusalem and destroyed the Temple. It was never rebuilt. All that remains today is the supporting wall of the Second Temple. The part that was nearest to the holiest place on the Temple Mount is called the Western Wall, or simply the Wall. In Hebrew, it is called the *Kotel*.

WHAT DO YOU THINK?

Synagogue is from a Greek word that means "a place of gathering." Do you think this is a good word to describe a place where Jews worship? Why or why not? Do you prefer another word? Why?

When you visit Israel, you can go to the Western Wall. It is a place for prayer, for remembering our long history, and for feeling hopeful about our future.

A Princess Among the Other Lands

On Tisha B'Av, the holiday on which we mourn the destruction of the Temple in Jerusalem, we read the Book of Lamentations. This book is a series of sad poems that tell of the destruction of Jerusalem. Read the following lines from Lamentations.

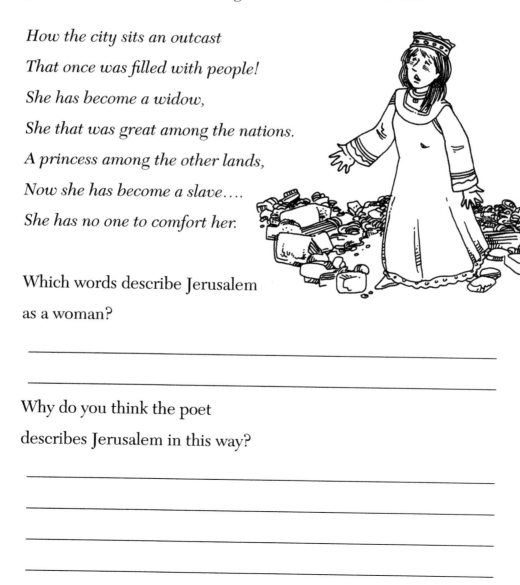

How the city sits an outcast
That once was filled with people!
She has become a widow,
She that was great among the nations.
A princess among the other lands,
Now she has become a slave….
She has no one to comfort her.

Which words describe Jerusalem as a woman?

_____

_____

Why do you think the poet describes Jerusalem in this way?

_____

_____

_____

_____

In the space below, draw a picture of how Jerusalem might have looked as "a princess among the other lands" before the destruction of the Temple. Use your imagination.

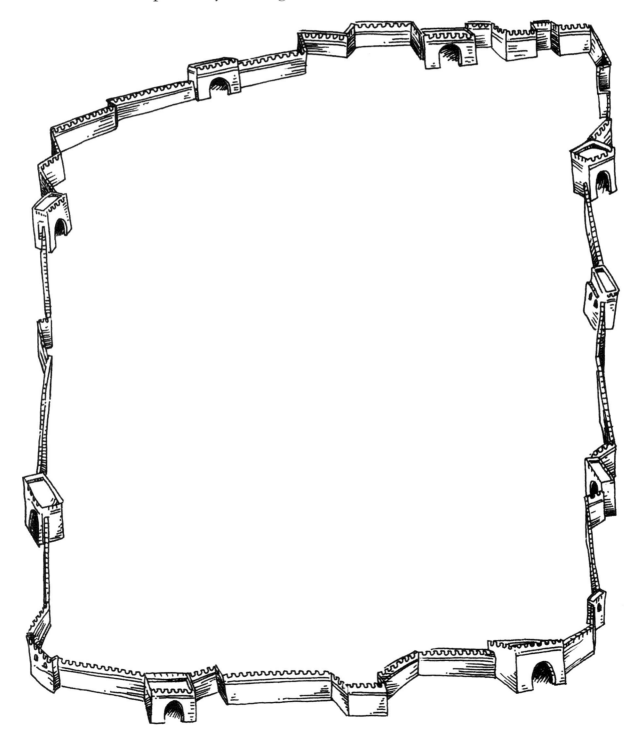

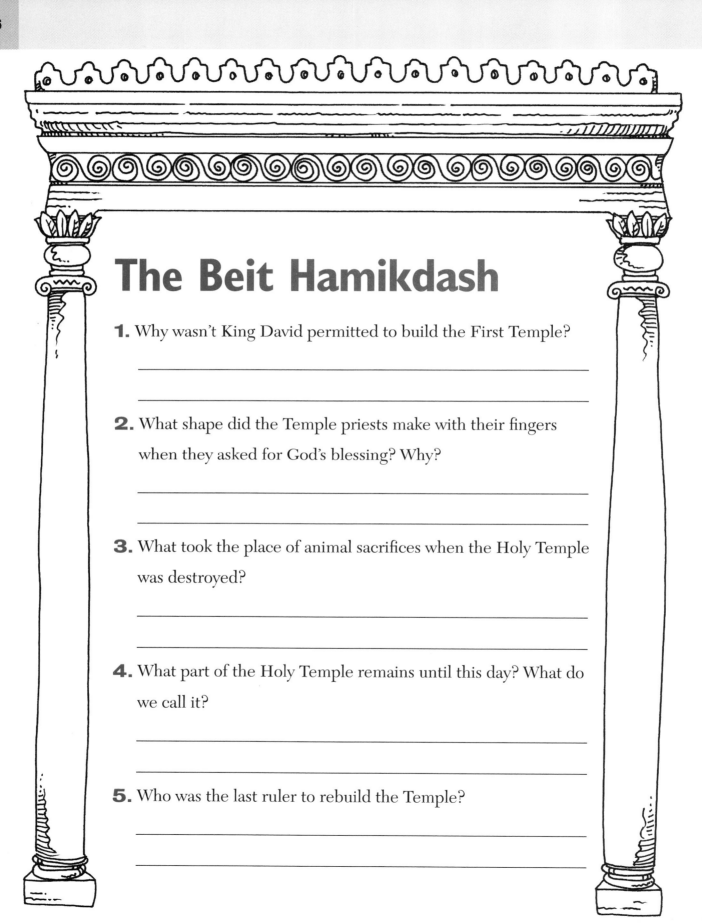

The Beit Hamikdash

1. Why wasn't King David permitted to build the First Temple?

_____

_____

2. What shape did the Temple priests make with their fingers when they asked for God's blessing? Why?

_____

_____

3. What took the place of animal sacrifices when the Holy Temple was destroyed?

_____

_____

4. What part of the Holy Temple remains until this day? What do we call it?

_____

_____

5. Who was the last ruler to rebuild the Temple?

_____

Synagogues
Around the World

Fasten your seat belts, because we are going around the world to look at synagogues. Each synagogue may look different, but all of them are houses of worship in which our people come together to pray, study, and meet with one another.

CENTERS OF JEWISH LIFE

After the Second Temple was destroyed, Jews built houses of worship — synagogues — wherever they settled. These houses of worship became centers of Jewish life.

The word *center* is very important. Look at these two pictures.

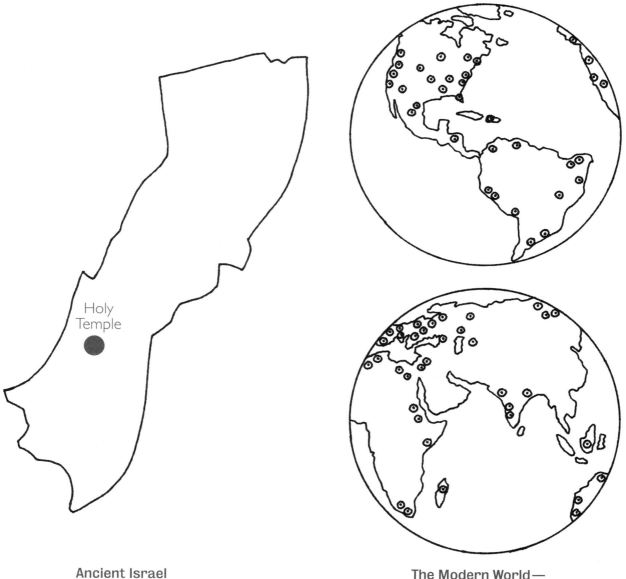

Ancient Israel

Holy Temple

The Modern World— Eastern and Western Hemispheres

The drawing of ancient Israel on page 28 represents Jewish life in the days of the First Temple. At that time, most Jews lived in the Land of Israel and the Temple was the center for Jewish life. But after the Temple was destroyed, new centers of Jewish life arose. The small circles in the illustrations of the Modern World represent some of the places around the world where Jews now live. The dots represent the many synagogues that serve as centers for the Jewish people who live there.

Today, synagogues provide us with:

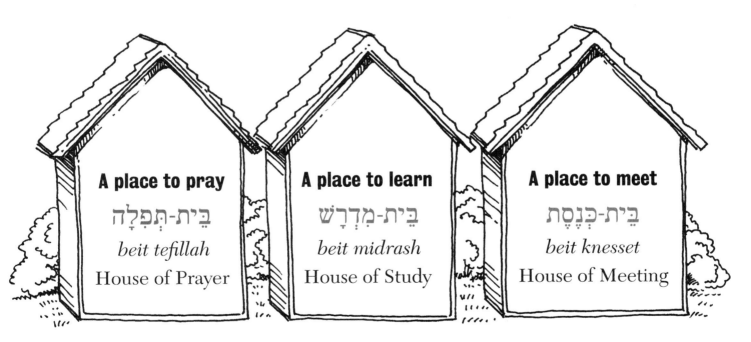

A place to pray

בֵּית-תְּפִלָּה

beit tefillah

House of Prayer

A place to learn

בֵּית-מִדְרָשׁ

beit midrash

House of Study

A place to meet

בֵּית-כְּנֶסֶת

beit knesset

House of Meeting

What Does a Synagogue

After the destruction of the First Temple, our people began to build synagogues in communities that had Jewish populations. What did these synagogues look like? Imagine houses in different countries, or even in different areas of your own city or town. Some houses have several levels. Others have only one level. Some houses have five bedrooms. Others have only one or two rooms in which to sleep. But all houses are places in which we eat, sleep, and relax with our families.

It is the same with synagogues. They may look different from one another, but each is built to serve the same purpose, to provide a place to talk to God *(beit tefillah),* a place to study about Judaism *(beit midrash),* and a place to meet with other Jews *(beit knesset).* Let us look at different synagogues around the world.

THE OLD SYNAGOGUE, WORMS, GERMANY
In the 11th century, Worms was a center of Jewish learning. The famous sage Rashi was one of the teachers who lived there. The Old Synagogue was built in 1034. It was destroyed during World War II and rebuilt in 1961. Few Jews now live in Worms, so today the synagogue is used as a museum.

ARCADIA SYNAGOGUE, PRETORIA, SOUTH AFRICA
Jewish scientists and mapmakers contributed to Vasco da Gama's discovery of the Cape of Good Hope in South Africa in 1497. But it was not until South Africa achieved religious tolerance in 1803 that Jewish settlers arrived in large numbers.

Look Like?

SYNAGOGUE IN KAIFENG, CHINA

The first Jews to live in China settled there 1,300 years ago. But the largest group arrived much later, during World War II, when Jews were forced to leave Japan, and German Jews came to escape the Holocaust. The model of the Kaifeng Synagogue shown here is based on an 18th-century drawing.

MAGEN DAVID SYNAGOGUE, BOMBAY, INDIA

Bene Israel, a community of Jews who live in India, trace their roots to the days of Judah Maccabee. At that time, the Greeks ruled Israel and forbade the study of Torah and the celebration of Shabbat. The Bene Israel claim their ancestors fled this oppression by sea. According to tradition, their boat was ship-wrecked near the coast of India, but fourteen survivors made it to shore and founded a community in Bombay.

MESGID, WOOZABA, ETHIOPIA

For more than 2,000 years the Jews of Ethiopia were completely cut off from the rest of the world. In fact, they believed they were the only Jews on earth! It was not until 1904 that they came into contact with the outside world. Since 1985, most Ethiopian Jews have resettled in Israel.

Pictured here is a *mesgid,* the place of worship and center of Jewish life for Ethiopian Jews.

TOURO SYNAGOGUE, RHODE ISLAND, U.S.A.

The U.S. Postal Service issued a stamp in 1982 honoring the Touro Synagogue, the oldest synagogue still standing in the United States. On the stamp were these words written in 1790 by George Washington to the Touro congregation: TO BIGOTRY, NO SANCTION. TO PERSECUTION, NO ASSISTANCE.

What Happens in Your "House"?

In some large synagogues, you may find all the activities listed below. In smaller synagogues, there may be only a few. Circle those activities that take place in your synagogue.

Jewish book fairs	Shabbat services
Hebrew classes	Ḥanukkah crafts fairs
Lectures	Swimming lessons
Passover seders	Cooking classes
Bible classes	Food collections for the poor
Fundraisers for the homeless	Basketball games
Youth clubs	Junior services

Other activities at your synagogue:

_____

_____

Describe one activity you enjoy at your synagogue.

_____

_____

Do you agree or disagree with this statement: It would be more difficult to live as a Jew if there were no synagogues. Explain your answer.

_____

_____

Where in the World Are These Synagogues?

After the destruction of the *Beit Hamikdash*, Jews were scattered all over the world. Unscramble the names of the five countries below, and you will see some of the places where Jews have built synagogues.

The Great Synagogue in
_ _ _ _ _ _

A E L I S R

DNAPOL

Zabludow Synagogue in
_ _ _ _ _ _

Aleppo Synagogue in
_ _ _ _ _

SYAIR

SATRAIULA

Bevis Marks Synagogue in
_ _ _ _ _ _ _

ANEGLND

Toorak Synagogue in
_ _ _ _ _ _ _ _ _

Tell Us About Your House

1. What is the name of your synagogue? If the name is in Hebrew, what does it mean in English?

_____

_____

2. When was your synagogue built?

_____

3. What is the most beautiful part of your synagogue? Why do you think so?

_____

_____

4. Imagine that your synagogue is being honored, like the Touro Synagogue, through the creation of a U.S. postage stamp. Draw a picture of the outside of your synagogue in the space below. And write the words you would want to appear on it.

The Sanctuary

Tall synagogues, small synagogues, stone synagogues, brick synagogues, Reform synagogues, Conservative synagogues, Orthodox synagogues, and Reconstructionist synagogues. What makes all these synagogues the same no matter where they are in the world?

Objects Found in a

Certain objects are found in almost every synagogue's sanctuary, the main room where people gather to pray. This is true no matter how large or small the synagogue is, no matter what materials the building is made of, and no matter what kind of Jews pray there.

מָגֵן-דָּוִד
Magen David
Star of David

פָּרֹכֶת
parochet
curtain

אֲרוֹן-קֹדֶשׁ
Aron Kodesh
Holy Ark

בִּימָה
bimah
stage

Synagogue Sanctuary

חַלּוֹנוֹת
ḥalonot
windows

סִדּוּר
siddur
prayer book

סֵפֶר תּוֹרָה
Sefer Torah
Torah Scroll

מְנוֹרָה
menorah
candelabrum

נֵר תָּמִיד
ner tamid
eternal light

אֲרוֹן-קֹדֶשׁ
Aron Kodesh
Holy Ark

The *Aron Kodesh* usually is located on the sanctuary wall facing Jerusalem. In North America, it is the eastern wall. When the congregation faces the *Aron Kodesh*, they are also facing Jerusalem.

Torah Scrolls—on which the Five Books of Moses are written—are kept in the *Aron Kodesh*. A representation of the

There are two pictures of the Torah on the doors of this *Aron Kodesh*. What is the difference between them?

two tablets of the Ten Commandments is often on the doors of the *Aron Kodesh* or, sometimes, above them or next to them.

in your synagogue

What design is on the doors of your synagogue's *Aron Kodesh*? Why do you think that design was chosen?

פָּרֹכֶת
parochet
curtain

Our tradition teaches that setting something apart can help make it holy. For example, the seventh day of the week, Shabbat, is set apart from the other days to help keep it holy. To show their love and respect for the Torah, many Ashkenazic Jews (Jews who come from central and eastern Europe) keep the Torah separated not only by the doors of the *Aron Kodesh* but also by hanging a beautiful curtain, called a *parochet*.

In the Book of Exodus, we are told how Moses "brought the Ark into the sanctuary and put up the curtain and screened the Ark." At the time of the Temple, a similar curtain was used to separate the Holy of Holies from the rest of the Temple.

The *parochet* that hangs in front of the *Aron Kodesh* is often colorful and beautifully embroidered. On the High Holidays (Rosh Hashanah and Yom Kippur), an all-white *parochet* is usually hung. In Judaism, the color white symbolizes purity and humility.

WHAT DO YOU THINK?

Why do you think it is the tradition to hang a white *parochet* in front of the *Aron Kodesh* during the High Holidays?

in your synagogue

Does the *Aron Kodesh* in your synagogue have a *parochet* hanging in front of it? If it does, of what material is it made? What design does it have?

The Hebrew words that are embroidered on this *parochet* are from the Book of Exodus. They mean, "But the bush was not consumed." Which character in the Bible saw a bush burning, but the bush was not burned up? Hint: That person led the Israelites out of Egypt. Why do you think these words were embroidered on the *parochet*? What words might you put on a *parochet* if you made one?

What time of year would this white *parochet* be hung? Hint: The Hebrew words at the top mean "Open the gates of heaven to our prayer."

נֵר תָּמִיד
ner tamid
eternal light

There is a light in the synagogue that is never turned off. In Hebrew, it is called the *ner tamid,* which means the "always light." The *ner tamid* remains lit both day and night, always.

In English, it is called the eternal light. Every synagogue in the world has one. It shines from the top of the Ark, reminding us that God is always with us even when there is darkness in our lives.

Ancient synagogues used oil in the *ner tamid.* Later on, tallow and wax candles were used. Today, we use electricity. But, no matter what is used to light a *ner tamid,* the light remains shining at all times.

Did You Know?

Do you know why people started using candles instead of oil in the *ner tamid*? Oil lamps created too much smoke in the synagogue, so people switched to tallow and wax candles. Eventually, synagogues began to use gas and then electric lights, because they were safer and more convenient.

in your synagogue

Describe the *ner tamid* in your synagogue.

Find the *ner tamid* in this picture. What is the *Aron Kodesh* shaped like? Why do you think that shape was chosen?

בִּימָה
bimah
stage

The raised platform in the sanctuary is called the *bimah*, which means "stage" in Hebrew. The moment you enter the sanctuary, you will see the *bimah*. The rabbi and the cantor usually lead prayer services from there. In most congregations, the Torah is read from the *bimah*. However, some congregations use a reading platform in the middle of the sanctuary instead.

in your synagogue

Does your congregation read the Torah from the *bimah* or from a reading platform in the middle of the sanctuary?

The Torah is usually read from a table on the *bimah*. At the Synagogue for the Deaf in Los Angeles, California, the Torah is held up as it is read, and someone translates the words into sign language. Which person is "signing" the Torah portion?

The menorah is the most ancient of all Jewish symbols in the synagogue. It is first mentioned in the Book of Exodus, when God commands Moses to make a menorah of pure gold. In ancient times, the menorah remained lit all the time in the Tent of Meeting. It had three branches on each side plus one in the middle—seven branches in all. Later, when the Temple was built in Jerusalem, the menorah stood in the Temple's sanctuary.

The Torah uses words like petals, blossoms, and branches to describe the appearance of the menorah. They are words that make us think of trees and plants.

Over the years, the menorah became a symbol of Judaism. Today, many sanctuaries have a menorah. When the modern state of Israel was created, its founders chose the menorah to be the official emblem of the country.

Mosaic art is made of small pieces of colored stone or glass. The menorah in this ancient mosaic looks similar to the one that stood in the Holy Temple. It too has seven branches and three legs.

Did You Know?

What is the difference between the menorah that was made for the Temple and the menorah, or ḥanukkiah, that we light on Ḥanukkah? The menorah in the Temple had seven branches. A Ḥanukkah menorah has nine branches — eight branches for the eight days of Ḥanukkah and a ninth branch, the *shammash*, or helper candle, that is used to light the other candles.

in your synagogue

Is there a menorah in your sanctuary? What does it look like? Does it hold candles?

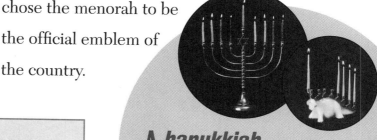

A ḥanukkiah can come in any color, size, or shape, but every ḥanukkiah must have nine branches. Which of these two ḥanukkiot (plural of ḥanukkiah) was lit on the fourth day of Ḥanukkah? Which was lit on the eighth day? How do you know?

מָגֵן-דָּוִד
Magen David
Star of David

Unlike the menorah, the *Magen David* is not mentioned anywhere in the Torah. *Magen David* means "Shield of David." However, in English it is usually called the "Star of David." It is a six-pointed star. Some people say King David's shield was in the shape of a star, and that is how the name came to be. No one knows for sure.

Today, the *Magen David* appears in most synagogues. It is the emblem on the Israeli flag. And, just as many countries have first-aid organizations like the Red Cross, Israel's ambulances and clinics are known as the *Magen David Adom*, the Red Shield of David.

in your synagogue

How many *Magen David* symbols are in your synagogue's sanctuary? Where are they located?

This Israeli ambulance belongs to the *Magen David Adom*, the Red Shield of David. Just like the American Red Cross, the *Magen David Adom* provides emergency medical help. Why do you think it is called the Red Shield of David?

חַלוֹנוֹת
halonot
windows

The Talmud—the set of holy books that contain Jewish law—teaches that "One should only pray in a house with windows." The windows are meant to remind us that there is a world beyond the sanctuary, a world in which work must be done and in which the sick and needy must be helped.

Over time, windows became works of art. Stained-glass windows often include designs of lions, snakes, trees, birds, and symbols of the twelve tribes of Israel.

The artist Marc Chagall created twelve stained-glass windows for the synagogue at Hadassah Hospital in Jerusalem. Each window honors one of the twelve tribes of Israel. This Israeli postage stamp shows the window that honors Joseph.

in your synagogue

Does your synagogue have decorated windows in the sanctuary? Describe them.

WHAT DO YOU THINK?

Why do you think it is important to remember the world of our deeds when we pray?

סִדּוּר
siddur
prayer book

We pray in the synagogue sanctuary, but how do we know what words to say?

We use a siddur. A siddur is a book that helps us talk to God. It includes many prayers that our people have offered to God over thousands of years, from ancient times to the present. While the siddur that is used in your synagogue may be different from the one that is used in your friend's synagogue, all siddurim (plural of siddur) contain a set order of prayers for the weekdays, Shabbat, and holidays. In fact, the word *siddur* means "order."

This family is praying together at Shabbat services in the synagogue. They are reading from a siddur. Some prayers in the siddur are ancient. For example, the words of the Shma prayer come from the Torah. Other prayers are modern— for example, those for the State of Israel.

סֵפֶר תּוֹרָה
Sefer Torah
Torah Scroll

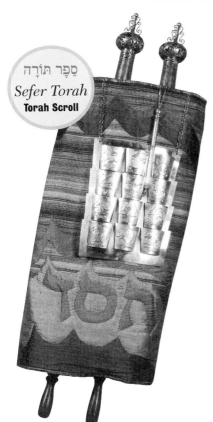

Most synagogues have at least two Torah Scrolls. When a *Sefer Torah* is taken out of, or returned to, the Ark, the congregation stands to show respect. In the next chapter, we will learn more about how we show our love and respect for the Torah.

in **your** synagogue

What is the name of the siddur your synagogue uses?

What's in a Name?

Objects that are found in the sanctuary of a synagogue have Hebrew and English names. Connect the English words in the left column to the matching Hebrew word in the right column.

ENGLISH	HEBREW
Eternal Light	Menorah
Prayer Book	Magen David
Holy Ark	Aron Kodesh
Candelabrum	Ner Tamid
Windows	Siddur
Star of David	Halonot

Use the Hebrew words above to complete this paragraph.

Jesse sat in the sanctuary. Above the _____ _____ (where the Torah is kept) hung the _____ _____. On the *bimah* was the _____, which looked like a tree with seven branches. Jesse looked at the stained-glass _____. He saw a six-pointed _____ _____ on the design. He took a book called a _____ that contains the prayer service.

In the Sanctuary

1. Why does the *ner tamid* burn day and night?

_____

_____

2. Which direction do you face when you stand before the *Aron Kodesh*? What is the importance of this direction?

_____

_____

3. Why does the *Aron Kodesh* sometimes have a *parochet*?

_____

_____

4. Where was the original menorah kept in ancient Jerusalem? How many branches did it have?

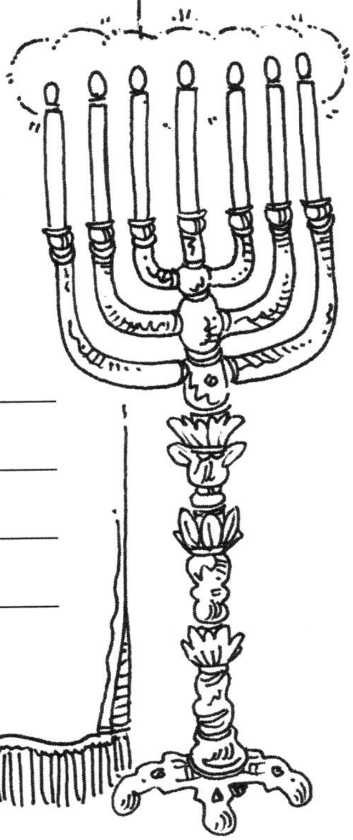

_____

_____

5. How many of the objects described in this chapter are in your synagogue? List them below.

_____

_____

_____

_____

Let the Sun Shine In

Use the space below to design a stained-glass window for your synagogue's sanctuary. Before beginning your design, think about the Jewish symbols you would like to include.

The Torah

Do you know what is inside every synagogue in the world, from Boston to Shanghai? It is a treasure beyond compare, both a gift and a responsibility. It is the Torah. But why is it so important to the Jewish people?

HOW THE TORAH IS ORGANIZED

The Torah is like a family album. Through its many stories, we have a "picture" of the first mothers and fathers of the Jewish people. In the Torah, you can read about Abraham and Sarah, Isaac and Rebecca, and Jacob, Leah, and Rachel. You can read about Joseph and his ornamented coat and about Moses leading the children of Israel to the Promised Land. In the Torah, you can also read about God's commandments — mitzvot — which teach us how to live as Jews.

The Torah is divided into five sections, or books. Each book has its own name.

READING THE TORAH

The Torah is divided into fifty-four portions. Each week, one portion is read in the synagogue, except during certain years when two portions are combined several times in the year. In this way, we read the entire Torah each year. On the day we read the last portion of Deuteronomy, it is the tradition to continue with the beginning of Genesis. We do this on the holiday of Simḥat Torah, to show our joy in beginning the reading of the Torah once again.

Did You Know?

The holiday that celebrates the completion of the year's Torah reading and the return to the beginning is called Simḥat Torah, which means "Rejoicing in the Torah." Do you know the name of the holiday that celebrates the giving of the Torah to the Jewish people at Mount Sinai? Hint: This holiday comes fifty days after the first day of Passover.

On Simḥat Torah, many synagogues welcome new students to the tradition of Jewish learning by holding a ceremony called a "consecration." Often, the rabbi recites a blessing over the students and gives each one a certificate or gift.

HOW DO YOU MAKE A TORAH?

Hundreds of years ago, books were written on parchment—the tanned skin of an animal—and were called scrolls. Today, the Torah is still written on parchment made from the skin of a kosher animal, usually a sheep. In most ways, every Torah Scroll must be exactly the same as every other Torah Scroll. In other ways, each Torah Scroll, or *Sefer Torah,* can have its own personality.

What Must Be the Same?

✔ Every Torah Scroll must have the same words in the same order.

✔ Every Torah Scroll must be written on parchment made from a kosher animal.

✔ Every Torah Scroll must be written by a scribe, called a *sofer*.

✔ Every Torah Scroll must be written with a quill pen or a reed, and special ink.

✔ Every Torah Scroll must be written in Hebrew.

In addition, we are not permitted to use a Torah Scroll that has mistakes in it. Why? Because a mistake would change the Torah. Our tradition teaches that we must not change the Torah. In fact, if any of the rules for making a Torah Scroll are not followed, we cannot use the Scroll.

A *sofer*, or scribe, must work carefully to follow strictly the rules for creating a *Sefer Torah*. It can take a *sofer* up to one year to complete a Torah Scroll.

This *sofer* is repairing a Torah Scroll that is worn from use.

What Can Be Different?

In the *Aron Kodesh* in your synagogue, you may find more than one *Sefer Torah*. One Scroll may be large and another small. One may be heavy and another light. Each Scroll may be "dressed" differently from the others, with a covering made of different colors and its own design. Some Scrolls may have crowns on the top; some may not. But inside each Scroll are the exact same words in the exact same order.

Recipe for One Torah Scroll, Well Done

1. Make parchment by soaking the skin of a kosher animal until the hair falls off. Then, stretch, scrape, and sand the skin until it is smooth enough to write on.

2. Make ink from blackberry juice, plus ground-up charcoal and iron.

3. Make a quill pen from the feather of a turkey or a goose, or a split reed.

4. Use a *sargel*, a tool made with a thorn, to scratch writing lines onto the parchment before you begin writing. This will help you keep all the margins the same and all the lines straight.

5. Now you are ready to write… almost. You must check every letter of every word against other Torah texts to prevent mistakes. And you must say each word three times before writing it.

Recipe for One Torah Scroll, Well Done

6. If you make an error, scrape it off with a blade and pumice stone. But, if you misspell God's name, that piece of parchment cannot be used.

7. Check and double-check. Find a partner. Read the Scroll to your partner letter by letter from beginning to end—all 248 columns on 60 to 80 pieces of parchment. (Remember, if even one letter on a Scroll is incorrect, the Scroll can't be used.) You must do this three times. Then count the words in each of the five books that make up the Torah Scroll to make sure the correct number of words are there.

8. Use animal sinew (tendon) as thread to sew the parchment pieces together. Attach the parchment to the wooden rollers that turn the Scroll.

Guess how long, working six days a week, it takes to complete one Torah Scroll? About one year!

Did You Know?

What do you do with a piece of parchment that cannot be used because of an error? You store it in a *genizah*. A *genizah* is a storeroom for holy books that are worn out and for scrolls with errors on them. Why do we use a *genizah* instead of throwing out these books and scrolls? Because our tradition teaches us that anything that has God's name on it must be cared for with respect.

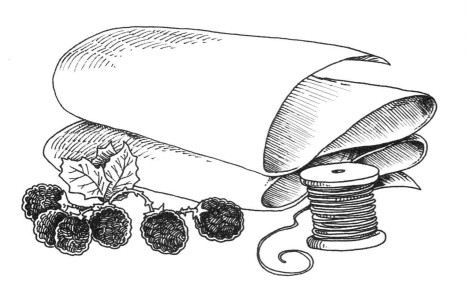

All Dressed Up

Here is what a well-dressed *Sefer Torah* wears.

רִמּוֹנִים
rimonim
headpieces

כֶּתֶר
keter
crown

חֹשֶׁן
ḥoshen
breastplate

יָד
yad
pointer or hand

חֲגוֹרָה
ḥagorah
binder, belt

מְעִיל
me'il
mantle

עֲצֵי-חַיִּים
atzei ḥayyim
trees of life, wooden rollers

58

כֶּתֶר
keter
crown

רִמּוֹנִים
rimonim
headpieces

Some Torah Scrolls wear a *keter,* or crown, as a symbol of royalty, just as kings and queens do.

Instead of a *keter,* some Torah Scrolls wear *rimonim.* Bells hang from the *rimonim* so that when you lift the Torah, you hear a soft tinkling. This sound signals the congregation to stand, out of respect for the Torah.

There are five Torah Scrolls in this Ark. How many are crowned with a *keter?* How many are crowned with *rimonim?*

Did You Know?

Rimonim is the Hebrew word for "pomegranates." Pomegranates are juicy red fruits that have many seeds. Some people say that when you open a pomegranate you find 613 seeds. Similarly, when you open the Torah, you find the 613 mitzvot that God gave us.

Another name for the Torah is "Tree of Life." The *rimonim,* or pomegranates, on a Torah are the "fruits" of the Tree of Life. Does this pomegranate remind you of the bells on *rimonim?*

in your synagogue

How many Torah Scrolls are there in your synagogue's *Aron Kodesh?* Are they all the same size? Do they wear a *keter* or two *rimonim?* Describe them.

יָד
yad
**pointer
or hand**

A chain hangs from a *Sefer Torah*. Attached to it is a pointer made of ivory, olive wood, or silver. The pointer has a tiny hand with a finger that points at the end. We use this hand, or *yad,* to help us keep our place when we read from the Scroll. We do not use our fingers to follow the words because oil or dirt from our skin could soil the parchment or smudge the ink.

Ashkenazic Jews (Jews who come from central and eastern Europe) make the *yad* with the index finger pointing on the right hand. That is the finger a ring is placed on during a traditional marriage ceremony. Sephardic Jews (Jews whose families come from Spain and Portugal) use a *yad* with an open hand as a symbol of good luck.

When we read from the *Sefer Torah,* a *yad* helps us keep our place so that we do not skip a word or line. It also helps keep us from touching the Scroll so that we do not get it dirty.

in your synagogue

What is the *yad* in your synagogue made of?

חֹשֶׁן
ḥoshen
breastplate

A *ḥoshen*, which is sometimes called a *tas*, rests under the *yad.* Just as in ancient times when soldiers used shields and breastplates for protection, a *ḥoshen* protects the Torah. The breastplate may have a variety of decorations on it, such as a tree or an Ark with a Torah Scroll.

This silver *ḥoshen* was made in Germany in 1752.

in your synagogue

What design or picture does the *ḥoshen* or *tas* in your synagogue have on it? Why do you think the design or picture was chosen for the shield?

מְעִיל
me'il
mantle

Beneath the *ḥoshen* or *tas* is the *me'il,* which means "mantle." The *me'il* is a cloth cover that is often colorful. It may be embroidered or be a tapestry. On Rosh Hashanah and Yom Kippur, the Torah Scrolls wear white mantles. They remind us to turn to God and ask for forgiveness so that our sins can be "washed as white as snow."

In some synagogues the *Sefer Torah* is not clothed in a *me'il.* Instead, it is kept in a case made of wood decorated with leather or metal. The case opens up into two sections.

in your synagogue

Describe the mantle or case for your synagogue's Torah. If your synagogue has several Torah Scrolls, describe your favorite mantle or case.

This *Sefer Torah* is kept in a case made of wood decorated with metal.

חֲגוֹרָה
ḥagorah
binder, belt

A *Sefer Torah* needs a belt, or *ḥagorah,* to prevent the parchment from unrolling. The *ḥagorah* often has a buckle. The belt is put on when the Torah is rolled and ready to be dressed.

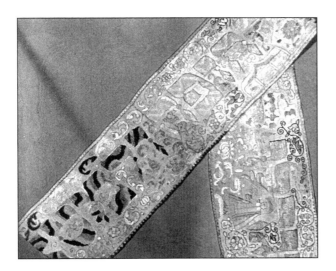

WHAT DO YOU THINK?

In some Ashkenazic communities, it was the custom to tie the Torah at a boy's bar mitzvah with a *ḥagorah* that was made out of the blanket in which he was wrapped at his *brit milah.* This type of *ḥagorah* is called a "wimpel."

Do you like this tradition? Why or why not? What else do you think would make a good belt for a *Sefer Torah*?

in your synagogue

Describe the belt on your synagogue's Torah Scroll.

עֲצֵי-חַיִּים
atzei ḥayyim
**trees of life,
wooden rollers**

The Torah Scroll is wrapped around two wooden rollers, *atzei ḥayyim*. Each roller is called a "tree of life," an *etz ḥayyim*.

Etz ḥayyim is also a name for the Torah. Just as the fruit, shade, and flowers from trees add strength, sweetness, and beauty to our lives, so the lessons and commandments of the Torah help us live strong, sweet, and happy lives.

This is a *megillah*—a Scroll of Esther—and a *yad*. The Scroll of Esther is much smaller than a Torah Scroll and has only one roller. When do we read the *megillah*? Why do you think it needs only one roller?

After the Torah portion is read, the *Sefer Torah* is raised up high so that the entire congregation can see it. The congregation stands up and sings, "This is the Torah that Moses placed before the people of Israel—God's word given through Moses."

Label It

Below is a fully dressed *Sefer Torah*.

Label the parts

Rimonim   **Ḥoshen**   **Me'il**   **Yad**   **Etz Ḥayyim**

Time to Get Dressed

Just as you put on your socks before your shoes, so a Torah Scroll must be dressed in a particular order. Look at the pictures below. Can you figure out the correct order of dressing the *Sefer Torah*? Number the pictures to show the order.

How We Pray

Y*ou know that a synagogue is a place of prayer.
But what is prayer, and why and how do we pray?*

TALKING TO GOD

What is prayer? Prayer is how we talk to God.

Why do we pray? Have you ever been filled with so much happiness that you wanted to burst? Have there been times when you were sad or angry or alone and didn't know where to turn for help? Did you talk to someone about your feelings? Did you talk to God?

When important things happen, prayer, or *tefillah,* תְּפִלָּה, can make us stop and think carefully about what is on our mind. *Tefillah* can comfort us when we are frightened, angry, hurt, or lonely, and it can express our joy when we are happy and thankful.

How do we talk to God? There is no one way to speak to God. When we are alone, we may speak to God silently from our hearts. When we are with our congregation, we usually talk to God through song and with prayers from a prayer book, or siddur.

Prayer can help turn our feelings of joy into words of thanks and appreciation. Prayer can also comfort us when we feel sad, frightened, or hurt. And prayer can remind us of God's love when we feel angry or lonely.

FOUR KINDS OF PRAYER

Most prayers fall into one of four groups.

Prayers of Thanks

There are heartfelt thank-yous we say to God for the goodness in the lives of our people. For example, we thank God for bringing us out of ancient Egypt and for parting the Sea of Reeds. And there are heartfelt thank-yous we say to God for the goodness in our personal lives. For example, we thank God for the food and health we enjoy.

Thanking God can sometimes feel like telling your Aunt Susan her matzah balls are delicious. You feel great not only because you've enjoyed yourself but also because you have expressed your appreciation.

Prayers of Request

Our tradition teaches us to pray for the willingness and strength to do our part to get what we want. For example, instead of praying for toys or CDs, we pray for the willingness to work and save for the things we want to buy. And, instead of praying for a good grade, we pray for the strength to study.

Prayers of Praise

We recite many prayers of praise that remind us of God's mercy, justice, goodness, and love. These prayers can give us hope when we are sad or frightened, and they can remind us of all the good in our lives.

Prayers of the Heart

When we talk to God like a friend, sharing the happy and the sad times, we may discover things we didn't know about ourselves and others. We may discover how much we love someone or realize how hurt someone we know is. We may discover that through acts of kindness, such as sending an e-mail message to someone who is sick or helping a parent prepare dinner, we can make a big difference in someone's life.

As you can see, prayer can be many things. But one thing prayer can never be is a magic wand. The only miracles that happen when we pray are the miracles of finding hope and strength to help ourselves and others.

Why Do We Pray?

Here are some reasons why people pray.

List two reasons why you pray.

1. _____

2. _____

To find out more about prayer, read the following story about Abigail and what she prayed for.

How to Pass a Test

Late one night, Abigail stood shivering by her bedroom window. *What if I fail the social studies test?* she thought, with a big lump in her throat. *Mrs. Kramer says we need to know the names of all the presidents and their major accomplishments. I'll never pass the test.*

Jamie says he's not worried. He plans to stay up studying until 5 AM the night before the test. My brain turns off like a light after 10 PM. Besides, Mrs. Kramer said that since the test isn't for another two weeks, we should study a little bit every day. But what if I learn a little bit one day and then forget it the next day? It's too much to learn. How will I ever pass the test?

Tears welled up in Abigail's eyes, and she began to pray.

Which of the following prayers could be helpful for Abigail to say?
Explain why.

A. Dear God, if You let me pass this exam,

I'll go to Shabbat services forever.

B. Dear God, please give me the patience to study

a little bit every day so that in two weeks I will

have learned what I need to know for the test.

C. Dear God, if You let me pass this exam,

I won't ever ask for anything else again.

D. Dear God, please have Mrs. Kramer cancel the test.

_____

_____

WE JUDGE OURSELVES

When we pray, we not only talk to God, we also talk to ourselves.
In fact, the Hebrew verb *l'hitpallel,* meaning "to pray," comes from
the same root as the Hebrew word that means "to judge yourself."
When we talk to God, we also judge ourselves. We know that we
lack something and ask God to help us.

For example, David prays, "Dear God, my little brother is
driving me crazy! Please help me be more patient." David has
judged himself. He knows that to become a better person, he
needs more patience, and for that he needs God's help.

TIME TO PRAY

To ensure that the Jewish people did not forget their relationship with God, the ancient rabbis created a schedule of daily prayer.

Shaḥarit	*morning service*
Musaf	*additional service, recited in some synagogues following Shaḥarit on Shabbat and festivals*
Minḥah	*afternoon service*
Ma'ariv	*evening service*

Ten adult Jews — a minyan — are required for a public prayer service. When you reach the age of bat or bar mitzvah (twelve or thirteen years old for a girl, thirteen for a boy) you may be counted in a minyan.

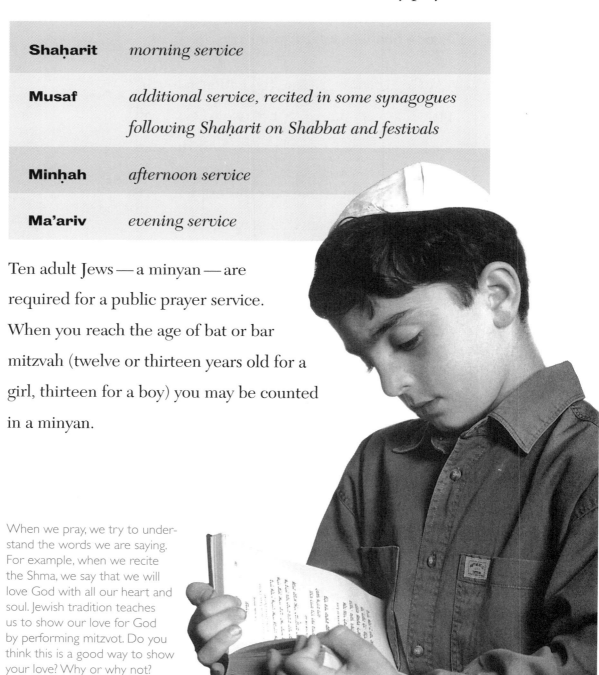

When we pray, we try to understand the words we are saying. For example, when we recite the Shma, we say that we will love God with all our heart and soul. Jewish tradition teaches us to show our love for God by performing mitzvot. Do you think this is a good way to show your love? Why or why not?

Why does our tradition encourage us to pray with our community rather than to pray alone? By praying with others, we are reminded that we are part of a much larger "family." In fact, most Jewish prayers are meant to be said when we pray as a community. That is why we say, "Blessed are You, *our* God," not "*my* God."

Even when we are alone, we say the same words that we recite with our congregation. We do this because we believe that a Jew is never alone when praying. Our prayers strengthen and unite us—in joy and in sorrow, in victory and in defeat, and in courage and in fear—with Jews throughout the world and throughout Jewish history.

This woman is a scuba diver. What is she wearing? Why must she wear special clothes and equipment?

THE PRAYING UNIFORM

What do nurses wear that help us identify them? What do police officers wear? Firefighters? Astronauts? Football players? Postal workers? Clowns? Chefs?

They all wear uniforms, clothes that help others identify the work they do, clothes that protect them and help them do their jobs better. What other people wear uniforms when they work? Do you think it is important that they wear their uniforms? Why or why not?

You probably wear uniforms too and know how helpful they can be. For example, if you take ballet lessons, you can dance more gracefully and comfortably wearing ballet shoes than swimming flippers. And, if you play team sports, your uniform can protect you and quickly help others identify which team you are on.

Here are some of the things we wear as a uniform when we pray. As you read, think about how they help us when we pray.

כִּפָּה
kippah
skullcap

A kippah is a small round cap worn on the head. Some people call it by its Yiddish name, *yarmulke*; others by its English name, skullcap. Some kippot (plural of kippah) are knitted, others crocheted, and yet others are made of velvet, silk, leather, and other materials. Some Jews wear kippot all the time; others wear them only when they pray or study holy books, such as the Bible and Talmud. And other Jews do not wear kippot at all.

How did the tradition of wearing a kippah begin? Judaism was born in the Middle East, where one sign of respect was for a man to cover his head in the presence of a high official or God.

Many people own several different kippot. They may receive them as gifts, for example, at a bar or bat mitzvah celebration or at a wedding. Or, they may buy them in their synagogue's Judaica shop. The kippot in this photograph are being sold in an open air market in Jerusalem.

טַלִּית
tallit
**prayer
shawl**

A tallit is a prayer shawl with long fringes, called *tzitzit*, attached to each corner. In the Torah, God says: "Wear the fringes to remember what I have done for you—when I took you out of Egypt and brought you to the Promised Land."

The *tzitzit* are knotted in a special way to represent the 613 mitzvot in the Torah. Just as some people tie a string around their fingers to help them remember something, when we look at the *tzitzit,* we are reminded to obey God's commandments.

Tallitot (plural of tallit) come in different colors and designs, but it is the tradition for all *tzitzit* to be white. In most synagogues, young people begin wearing a tallit when they reach the age of bar or bat mitzvah. Traditionally, women did not wear *tallitot,* but today many do.

When you are in bed at night, wrapped in warm blankets, you are ready to relax, sleep, and dream. When you put on the tallit, you are wrapped in the warmth and comfort of God's presence, ready to talk to God.

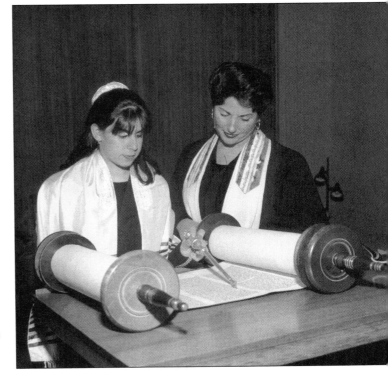

This girl is practicing for her bat mitzvah service. She is wearing a tallit that belongs to the synagogue. On the day of the service, before she reads from the Torah, her parents will present her with a tallit that was made specially for her.

תְּפִלִּין
tefillin
boxes with parchment

Tefillin are two small black leather boxes attached to black leather straps. As with a mezuzah, a parchment with verses from the Torah is placed inside each tefillin box. Tefillin are worn by many Jewish adults every morning, except on Shabbat and festival mornings. Like kippot and *tallitot*, until recently, only men put on tefillin. Today, some women put them on as well.

We are commanded to strap one leather box around our arm and the other around our head as a symbol of our faith in God. This commandment comes from the fifth book of the Torah, Deuteronomy. In Deuteronomy, we are told to bind the words from the Shma "as a sign upon your hand; let them be a symbol before your eyes."

When we put on tefillin, we say, "By this symbol, we bind hand, heart, and mind to the service of the Holy Blessed One."

WHAT DO YOU THINK?

Do you think it is helpful to dress in a special way when you pray to God? Why or why not? What do you like to wear in synagogue? Why?

CHALLENGE QUESTION: What are the duties of the people who lead prayer services in your synagogue? Find out in the next chapter.

This man is putting on ("laying") tefillin. What else is he wearing as part of his "prayer uniform"?

The Way We Pray

1. Why is praying in a group important to Jews?

_____

_____

_____

2. List three things for which you are thankful and three things you
   want. For example, you might list that you are thankful for the
   love of your family and that you want to take a trip somewhere.

   I am thankful for:

   1. _____

   2. _____

   3. _____

   I would like:

   1. _____

   2. _____

   3. _____

Look at the six items you listed in activity two on page 77 and decide which ones would be appropriate to include in a prayer. Then, write two personal prayers based on them. The first prayer should be a prayer of thanks and the second a prayer of request. Remember: prayer is not a magic wand!

My prayer of thanks:

_____

_____

_____

_____

My prayer of request:

_____

_____

_____

_____

Three Houses in One

What house contains three houses? The synagogue. The synagogue is a beit tefillah *(house of prayer)*, beit midrash *(house of study)*, and beit knesset *(house of meeting). Find out what these three "houses" are and how they make a glorious one!*

BEIT TEFILLAH

Beit tefillah means "house of prayer," a place where people pray. There are several people in the *beit tefillah* who lead us in our prayers! Do you know who they are? Read on to find out.

Take Me to Your Leader

Think about playing soccer. It is a group effort. On each team, there are members who play offense, members who play defense, and members who are goalies. There is also a coach as well as a referee.

A synagogue also requires a group effort. Some people have full-time jobs in the synagogue, others may work there part-time, and yet others may volunteer to help out when they can. Here are some of the many people who work in synagogues.

Rabbi The rabbi teaches classes in Bible, Jewish traditions, and Jewish history; visits people when they are sick; leads prayer services; and helps congregants observe holidays and special, personal events, such as weddings and baby namings.

Cantor The cantor leads the musical parts of the prayer service. The cantor may also teach classes and help children (and some adults!) prepare for their bat or bar mitzvah services.

Education Director The Education Director is in charge of the religious school and works with your teachers to help you learn to live as a Jew. In some synagogues, the Education Director is also in charge of adult and family education.

Ba'al Keriah or Ba'alat Keriah The *ba'al keriah* or, if it is a woman, *ba'alat keriah,* is the person who reads from the *Sefer Torah* during prayer services. That person may be the cantor, the rabbi, or a congregant. The Torah Scrolls have no vowels, or *nekudot,* and some letters have a slightly different shape than when they are printed in the siddur.

Gabbai The *gabbai* stands next to the person who reads the Torah during services. It is the *gabbai's* job to correct the reader's mistakes, if they are made.

The text above is from a Torah Scroll. Which Hebrew letters can you name? The first and sixth letter on the second line are *nuns*. (It may be familiar to you because it is one of the four letters on a dreidel.) Every *nun* in a *Sefer Torah* has a crown on top. Which other letters have crowns?

Congregants Every synagogue has members, or congregants, who help out in the synagogue. For example, congregants often volunteer in the religious school, assist in the planning or running of special events, such as book fairs, and serve as ushers during prayer services—greeting people and helping them find seats. Sometimes, when there is no rabbi or cantor present, a congregant may lead the prayer service. A congregant may also read from the Torah Scroll or perform the duties of the *gabbai*. What kind of volunteer work would you like to do in your synagogue?

The Rabbi

In what ways are teachers and rabbis the same?

1. A teacher listens to you. A rabbi does, too.

2. A teacher shares in your joy and comforts you when you feel sad. A rabbi does that, too—helping you celebrate happy events, such as a wedding or bat mitzvah celebration, and helping you face the difficult times, such as an illness or death in the family.

3. Teachers can be men or women. Rabbis can be men or women, too.

These students and their rabbi are standing on the *bimah* of their sanctuary. The rabbi is holding a shofar and teaching the children about Rosh Hashanah.

4. Teachers study to become professionals. Rabbis do also. Today, people become rabbis by studying in religious schools called seminaries after they have completed college. When they complete these studies, they are ordained as rabbis.

During Shabbat and holiday services, rabbis present sermons lessons from the Bible that teach us how to live as Jews.

In what ways are teachers and rabbis different?

1. Teachers usually work in a school. Rabbis work in many places—in synagogues, hospitals, nursing homes, and camps!

2. Teachers usually teach new students every year. Rabbis usually teach the same people for many years.

3. Teachers don't usually teach both children and adults. Rabbis usually teach all members of the community.

Printer's Errorr

Oops, the printer goofed. Please unjumble the words below to discover the names of people who lead prayer services in the *beit tefillah*. Complete the definitions by writing in the correctly spelled words.

BAGIBA   BABIR   ALTABA' EIRHAK   ROCATN

A _____ leads the musical portion of the service.

A _____ is a teacher, counselor, prayer leader, friend, and more.

A _____ makes sure that mistakes are corrected when the Torah Scrolls are read.

A _____ _____ is an expert trained in reading Torah.

This cantor is teaching the students *z'mirot*, songs to sing on holidays and Shabbat.

BEIT MIDRASH

In addition to being a house of prayer, a synagogue is also a school—not just for children but also for adults. *Beit midrash* means "house of study," a place where people come to learn about Judaism and how to live as Jews.

Religious school often begins with nursery school and continues through high school. Children usually attend classes in the afternoon and on weekends. They study Hebrew and Torah and learn about Jewish holidays, history, and values. Many communities also have day schools—full-time schools that combine Jewish studies with everyday subjects, such as math, English, social studies, and science. Some congregations have day-care programs as well.

Adults come to the synagogue to study, too. In the synagogue, they can study Hebrew and Torah and learn more about holiday observances and Jewish law, art, music, and cooking.

In religious school, we learn how to live as Jews. We also have fun and make new friends. What do you enjoy most about your school?

Many synagogues have libraries filled with Jewish books, videos, magazines, newspapers, encyclopedias, and CDs.

Who's Who in Your Synagogue?

Name of Synagogue: ———————————————

Name of Rabbi: ———————————————

Name of Cantor: ———————————————

Name of Synagogue President: ———————————————

Name of Education Director: ———————————————

Names of My Teachers: ———————————————

———————————————

Subjects I Study: ———————————————

———————————————

———————————————

My Favorite Subject Is: ———————————————

It is My Favorite Subject Because: ———————————————

———————————————

BEIT KNESSET

The *beit knesset* is the third "house" that makes up the synagogue. *Beit knesset* means "house of meeting." This name reminds us that the synagogue is a place where Jewish people meet in order to do things together.

Have you ever worn a costume to a synagogue Purim carnival? Or participated in a Passover seder at a synagogue? Have you ever been at a concert at your synagogue or attended a play there?

Congregants often meet in the synagogue to plan volunteer and social-action activities such as food drives for the hungry and demonstrations on behalf of the homeless. The synagogue is also a place where people gather for holiday parties and Oneg Shabbat celebrations (social gatherings after Shabbat services), as well as art shows, film festivals, and sports events.

The next two pages show classes and events that take place in a synagogue. Which two would you like to attend? Why?

_____

_____

_____

Describe another class or event you think should be offered and tell why. _____

_____

_____

_____

Synagogue

Tzedakah Drive

Help raise money for the homeless.
Donations of clothes, books and food
welcome. Monday evening 7:30 - 9:30 PM.

notice

ASIAN COOKING

Learn to cook in a wok, with easy,
kosher, tasty, low-fat Chinese and
Vietnamese recipes. Thursday 4-6PM.

Soup Kitchen Sunday

Please meet outside the synagogue if
you are interested in serving food at
the soup kitchen on Hudson Street.
Parents and children welcome.

Sunday afternoon from 11- 1 PM.

Announcements

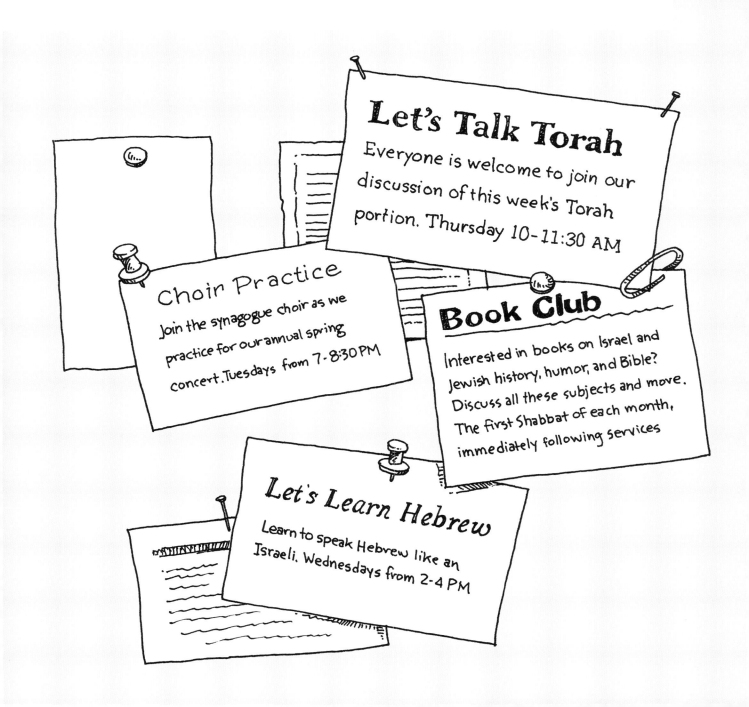

Let's Talk Torah
Everyone is welcome to join our discussion of this week's Torah portion. Thursday 10-11:30 AM

Choir Practice
Join the synagogue choir as we practice for our annual spring concert. Tuesdays from 7-8:30 PM

Book Club
Interested in books on Israel and Jewish history, humor, and Bible? Discuss all these subjects and more. The first Shabbat of each month, immediately following services

Let's Learn Hebrew
Learn to speak Hebrew like an Israeli. Wednesdays from 2-4 PM

WHAT A HOUSE!

"Mom? Guess what! I'm going to build a synagogue!" Danny called out when he came home.

"Really? That's a big job," answered his mom with a smile.

"It won't be a real one. I'm just going to design one on paper, and our Sunday school class is going to make a model of the winning plan. How should I start?"

"I would start by listing everything that goes on in a synagogue to make sure I leave space for all the activities."

"Good idea," Danny said. "You need a big place to pray, classrooms for school; there should be a big room for activities…and that's it!" Danny drew a diagram of his plan. "Here it is. Does it include everything a synagogue needs?"

After reviewing Danny's plan, his mom said, "The good part is that you have included some of the important places…but others are missing. For instance, who usually leads the prayer services?"

"The rabbi."

"Where is the rabbi's study?"

"*Umm*…I forgot."

"Does the rabbi pay the synagogue bills and send out the newsletter to the congregation?"

"I don't think so. Who does that?"

"The Executive Director. So you need at least one other office with room for a computer, printer, phone, fax, and copying machine."

"Okay. One more office coming up. And, that's all, folks!"

"Not so fast," Danny's mom said. "What does a school need to help teachers and students learn?"

"I know. A library."

"Absolutely," Danny's mom agreed. "And who runs the school?"

"The Education Director—who needs an office, too!"

"Of course," Mom said.

"And we'll need a room for school supplies. Are we done?" Danny asked.

"Not yet. You've got a big meeting room. What happens there?"

Danny explained, "The Brotherhood and Sisterhood have celebrations there like "Latke Night" at Ḥanukkah…and I've seen the youth group there collecting food to take to the hungry."

"So, tell me, where do the latkes come from?" Danny's mom asked.

"From potatoes," Danny replied. "Oh…you mean, the synagogue kitchen. And that reminds me of something else I forgot. The custodian needs a place for his cleaning supplies. Wow, there's a lot going on in one building."

"Yes, a synagogue is a very big home. A place for people to pray, learn, meet, and celebrate together. Somehow, if you have enough space for all that, there will be room for everyone."

Be an Architect

Imagine that you are an architect. Your assignment is to design a synagogue with enough rooms for the many people and activities that will take place there. Use the space below to make your floor plan. Don't forget to label each room.

CONCLUSION

A Light that Never Goes Out

As you read this book you learned how our ancestors journeyed through the wilderness, received the Torah at Mount Sinai, entered the Promised Land, and built the Temple. You learned about the synagogue, the meaning of prayer, and the many activities that occur in a synagogue. But where do you fit in?

ADDING LIGHT

Remember the *ner tamid* — the "always" light? Being a Jew is very much like being a human *ner tamid*, because we each can help the light of Judaism to continue burning, always.

Think about it. Our ancestors, who made altars to God, first lit that light. Moses, who brought the children of Israel through the wilderness, kept that light burning. And, when God gave us the Torah and asked us to build the Temple, the light continued to shine brightly.

When the First Temple was destroyed, the *ner tamid* within us continued to shine. We moved to other countries and built synagogues for worship, study, and meetings. Even when the Second Temple was destroyed, the *ner tamid* kept burning brightly. Why? Because each of us carries it inside ourselves.

When you perform a mitzvah—such as attending a Passover seder, giving tzedakah, or helping a parent—your light adds to the brightness of Judaism.

You have the power and the responsibility to keep your inner light shining. Others can join you. But no one can do your part for you. In the synagogue, you can strengthen those around you and be strengthened by them. Like you, they are working to keep the flame of Judaism burning brightly. שָׁלוֹם וּבְרָכָה, *shalom uvrachah*.

Peace be with you, and may you be blessed.

WELCOME TO OUR SYNAGOGUE

You have now concluded your study of the synagogue—its history; its ritual objects; and how it serves as a house of prayer, a house of study, and a house of meeting. In addition, you have thought about the special qualities of your own synagogue.

Write a message on the billboard below to welcome the community to your synagogue.